Great Works Instructional Guides for Literature

Hi! Fly Guy

A guide for the book by Tedd Arnold
Great Works Author: Tracy Pearce

Publishing Credits

Owen Pearce, *Contributing Author*

Image Credits

Timothy J. Bradley (cover; pages 11, 22); J.J. Rudisill (pages 45, 59–61)

Standards

© 2007 Teachers of English to Speakers of Other Languages, Inc. (TESOL)
© 2007 Board of Regents of the University of Wisconsin System. World-Class Instructional Design and Assessment (WIDA)
© Copyright 2010. National Governors Association Center for Best Practices and Council of Chief State School Officers. All rights reserved.

Shell Education

5301 Oceanus Drive
Huntington Beach, CA 92649-1030
http://www.shelleducation.com

ISBN 978-1-4258-8956-2

© 2014 Shell Educational Publishing, Inc.

The classroom teacher may reproduce copies of materials in this book for classroom use only. The reproduction of any part for an entire school or school system is strictly prohibited. No part of this publication may be transmitted, stored, or recorded in any form without written permission from the publisher.

Table of contents

How to Use This Literature Guide 4
    Theme Thoughts 4
    Vocabulary 5
    Analyzing the Literature 6
    Reader Response 6
    Guided Close Reading 6
    Making Connections 7
    Language Learning 7
    Story Elements 7
    Culminating Activity 8
    Comprehension Assessment 8
    Response to Literature 8

Correlation to the Standards 8
    Purpose and Intent of Standards 8
    How to Find Standards Correlations 8
    Standards Correlation Chart 9
    TESOL and WIDA Standards 10

About the Author— Tedd Arnold 11
    Possible Texts for Text Comparisons 11
    Cross-Curricular Connection 11

Book Summary of *Hi! Fly Guy* 12
    Possible Texts for Text Sets 11

Teacher Plans and Student Pages 13
    Pre-Reading Theme Thoughts 13
    Section 1: Chapter 1 14
    Section 2: Chapter 2 27
    Section 3: Chapter 3 37
    Section 4: Whole Book 49

Post-Reading Activities 58
    Post-Reading Theme Thoughts 58
    Culminating Activity: The Adventures of Fly Guy and Buzz 59
    Culminating Activity: Reader's Theater—Fly Guy Goes to the Fair 62
    Comprehension Assessment 65
    Response to Literature: Fly Guy and Buzz Meet 67

Writing Paper 70

Answer Key 71

Introduction

How to Use This Literature Guide

Today's standards demand rigor and relevance in the reading of complex texts. The units in this series guide teachers in a rich and deep exploration of worthwhile works of literature for classroom study. The most rigorous instruction can also be interesting and engaging!

Many current strategies for effective literacy instruction have been incorporated into these instructional guides for literature. Throughout the units, text-dependent questions are used to determine comprehension of the book as well as student interpretation of the vocabulary words. The books chosen for the series are complex and are exemplars of carefully crafted works of literature. Close reading is used throughout the units to guide students toward revisiting the text and using textual evidence to respond to prompts orally and in writing. Students must analyze the story elements in multiple assignments for each section of the book. All of these strategies work together to rigorously guide students through their study of literature.

The next few pages describe how to use this guide for a purposeful and meaningful literature study. Each section of this guide is set up in the same way to make it easier for you to implement the instruction in your classroom.

Theme Thoughts

The great works of literature used throughout this series have important themes that have been relevant to people for many years. Many of the themes will be discussed during the various sections of this instructional guide. However, it would also benefit students to have independent time to think about the key themes of the book.

Before students begin reading, have them complete the *Pre-Reading Theme Thoughts* (page 13). This graphic organizer will allow students to think about the themes outside the context of the story. They'll have the opportunity to evaluate statements based on important themes and defend their opinions. Be sure to keep students' papers for comparison to the *Post-Reading Theme Thoughts* (page 58). This graphic organizer is similar to the pre-reading activity. However, this time, students will be answering the questions from the point of view of one of the characters in the book. They have to think about how the character would feel about each statement and defend their thoughts. To conclude the activity, have students compare what they thought about the themes before they read the book to what the characters discovered during the story.

Pre-Reading Activities

For each chapter covered in this literature guide, there are suggestions for how to introduce the text to students. Teachers share information in a visual format and ask students to evaluate the content. Students must use the information presented in the illustrations to discuss what they are about to read and make predictions about the story.

Introduction

How to Use This Literature Guide (cont.)

Vocabulary

Each teacher reference vocabulary overview page has definitions and sentences about how key vocabulary words are used in the section. These words should be introduced and discussed with students. Students will use these words in different activities throughout the book.

On some of the vocabulary student pages, students are asked to answer text-related questions about vocabulary words from the sections. The following question stems will help you create your own vocabulary questions if you'd like to extend the discussion.

- How does this word describe _____'s character?
- How does this word connect to the problem in this story?
- How does this word help you understand the setting?
- Tell me how this word connects to the main idea of this story.
- What visual pictures does this word bring to your mind?
- Why do you think the author used this word?

At times, you may find that more work with the words will help students understand their meanings and importance. These quick vocabulary activities are a good way to further study the words.

- Students can play vocabulary concentration. Make one set of cards that has the words on them and another set with the definitions. Then, have students lay them out on the table and play concentration. The goal of the game is to match vocabulary words with their definitions. For early readers or English language learners, the two sets of cards could be the words and pictures of the words.

- Students can create word journal entries about the words. Students choose words they think are important and then describe why they think each word is important within the book. Early readers or English language learners could instead draw pictures about the words in a journal.

- Students can create puppets and use them to act out the vocabulary words from the stories. Students may also enjoy telling their own character-driven stories using vocabulary words from the original stories.

Introduction

How to Use This Literature Guide (cont.)

Analyzing the Literature

After you have read each section with students, hold a small-group or whole-class discussion. Provided on the teacher reference page for each section are leveled questions. The questions are written at two levels of complexity to allow you to decide which questions best meet the needs of your students. The Level 1 questions are typically less abstract than the Level 2 questions. These questions are focused on the various story elements, such as character, setting, and plot. Be sure to add further questions as your students discuss what they've read. For each question, a few key points are provided for your reference as you discuss the book with students.

Reader Response

In today's classrooms, there are often great readers who are below average writers. So much time and energy is spent in classrooms getting students to read on grade level that little time is left to focus on writing skills. To help teachers include more writing in their daily literacy instruction, each section of this guide has a literature-based reader response prompt. Each of the three genres of writing is used in the reader responses within this guide: narrative, informative/explanatory, and opinion. Before students write, you may want to allow them time to draw pictures related to the topic. Book-themed writing paper is provided on page 70 if your students need more space to write.

Guided Close Reading

Within the first four sections of this guide, it is suggested that you closely reread a portion of the text with your students. The sections to be reread are described by location within the story since there are no page numbers in this book. After rereading the section, there are a few text-dependent questions to be answered by students. Working space has been provided to help students prepare for the group discussion. They should record their thoughts and ideas on the activity page and refer to it during your discussion. Rather than just taking notes, you may want to require students to write complete responses to the questions before discussing them with you.

Encourage students to read one question at a time and then go back to the text and discover the answer. Work with students to ensure that they use the text to determine their answers rather than making unsupported inferences. Suggested answers are provided in the answer key.

How to Use This Literature Guide (cont.)

Guided Close Reading (cont.)

The generic open-ended stems below can be used to write your own text-dependent questions if you would like to give students more practice.

- What words in the story support . . . ?
- What text helps you understand . . . ?
- Use the book to tell why _____ happens.
- Based on the events in the story, . . . ?
- Show me the part in the text that supports . . . .
- Use the text to tell why . . . .

Making Connections

The activities in this section help students make cross-curricular connections to mathematics, science, social studies, fine arts, or other curricular areas. These activities require higher-order thinking skills from students but also allow for creative thinking.

Language Learning

A special section has been set aside to connect the literature to language conventions. Through these activities, students will have opportunities to practice the conventions of standard English grammar, usage, capitalization, and punctuation.

Story Elements

It is important to spend time discussing what the common story elements are in literature. Understanding the characters, setting, plot, and theme can increase students' comprehension and appreciation of the story. If teachers begin discussing these elements in early childhood, students will more likely internalize the concepts and look for the elements in their independent reading. Another very important reason for focusing on the story elements is that students will be better writers if they think about how the stories they read are constructed.

In the story elements activities, students are asked to create work related to the characters, setting, or plot. Consider having students complete only one of these activities. If you give students a choice on this assignment, each student can decide to complete the activity that most appeals to him or her. Different intelligences are used so that the activities are diverse and interesting to all students.

Introduction

How to Use This Literature Guide (cont.)

Culminating Activity

At the end of this instructional guide is a creative culminating activity that allows students the opportunity to share what they've learned from reading the book. This activity is open ended so that students can push themselves to create their own great works within your language arts classroom.

Comprehension Assessment

The questions in this section require students to think about the book they've read as well as the words that were used in the book. Some questions are tied to quotations from the book to engage students and require them to think about the text as they answer the questions.

Response to Literature

Finally, students are asked to respond to the literature by drawing pictures and writing about the characters and stories. A suggested rubric is provided for teacher reference.

Correlation to the Standards

Shell Education is committed to producing educational materials that are research and standards based. As part of this effort, we have correlated all of our products to the academic standards of all 50 states, the District of Columbia, the Department of Defense Dependents Schools, and all Canadian provinces.

Purpose and Intent of Standards

Standards are designed to focus instruction and guide adoption of curricula. Standards are statements that describe the criteria necessary for students to meet specific academic goals. They define the knowledge, skills, and content students should acquire at each level. Standards are also used to develop standardized tests to evaluate students' academic progress. Teachers are required to demonstrate how their lessons meet standards. Standards are used in the development of all of our products, so educators can be assured they meet high academic standards.

How To Find Standards Correlations

To print a customized correlation report of this product for your state, visit our website at http://www.shelleducation.com and follow the online directions. If you require assistance in printing correlation reports, please contact our Customer Service Department at 1-877-777-3450.

correlation to the standards (cont.)

standards correlation chart

The lessons in this book were written to support the Common Core College and Career Readiness Anchor Standards. The following chart indicates which lessons address the anchor standards.

Common Core College and Career Readiness Anchor Standard	Section
CCSS.ELA-Literacy.CCRA.R.1—Read closely to determine what the text says explicitly and to make logical inferences from it; cite specific textual evidence when writing or speaking to support conclusions drawn from the text.	Guided Close Reading Sections 1–4; Story Elements Sections 1–4
CCSS.ELA-Literacy.CCRA.R.2—Determine central ideas or themes of a text and analyze their development; summarize the key supporting details and ideas.	Analyzing the Literature Sections 1–4; Guided Close Reading Sections 1–4; Making Connections Sections 3–4; Post-Reading Response to Literature
CCSS.ELA-Literacy.CCRA.R.3—Analyze how and why individuals, events, or ideas develop and interact over the course of a text.	Analyzing the Literature Sections 1–4; Guided Close Reading Sections 1–4; Story Elements Section 2; Post-Reading Response to Literature
CCSS.ELA-Literacy.CCRA.R.4—Interpret words and phrases as they are used in a text, including determining technical, connotative, and figurative meanings, and analyze how specific word choices shape meaning or tone.	Vocabulary Sections 1–4; Guided Close Reading Sections 1–4; Language Learning Section 1
CCSS.ELA-Literacy.CCRA.R.5—Analyze the structure of texts, including how specific sentences, paragraphs, and larger portions of the text (e.g., a section, chapter) relate to each other and the whole.	Vocabulary Sections 1–4; Guided Close Reading Sections 1–4
CCSS.ELA-Literacy.CCRA.R.7—Integrate and evaluate content presented in diverse media and formats, including visually and quantitatively, as well as in words.	Pre-Reading Activities Sections 1–3
CCSS.ELA-Literacy.CCRA.W.1—Write arguments to support claims in an analysis of substantive topics or texts using valid reasoning and relevant and sufficient evidence.	Reader Response Section 1
CCSS.ELA-Literacy.CCRA.W.2—Write informative/explanatory texts to examine and convey complex ideas and information clearly and accurately through the effective selection, organization, and analysis of content.	Reader Response Section 4
CCSS.ELA-Literacy.CCRA.W.3—Write narratives to develop real or imagined experiences or events using effective technique, well-chosen details, and well-structured event sequences.	Reader Response Sections 2–3; Story Elements Sections 1, 4

Introduction

Correlation to the Standards (cont.)

Standards Correlation Chart (cont.)

Common Core College and Career Readiness Anchor Standard	Section
CCSS.ELA-Literacy.CCRA.W.4—Produce clear and coherent writing in which the development, organization, and style are appropriate to task, purpose, and audience.	Reader Response Sections 1–4; Story Elements Sections 1, 4; Culminating Activity
CCSS.ELA-Literacy.CCRA.L.1—Demonstrate command of the conventions of standard English grammar and usage when writing or speaking.	Guided Close Reading Sections 1–4; Language Learning Sections 1, 3–4; Culminating Activity
CCSS.ELA-Literacy.CCRA.L.2—Demonstrate command of the conventions of standard English capitalization, punctuation, and spelling when writing.	Reader Response Sections 1–4; Language Learning Section 2
CCSS.ELA-Literacy.CCRA.L.3—Apply knowledge of language to understand how language functions in different contexts, to make effective choices for meaning or style, and to comprehend more fully when reading or listening.	Language Learning Section 1; Story Elements Section 4
CCSS.ELA-Literacy.CCRA.L.4—Determine or clarify the meaning of unknown and multiple-meaning words and phrases by using context clues, analyzing meaningful word parts, and consulting general and specialized reference materials, as appropriate.	Vocabulary Sections 1–4
CCSS.ELA-Literacy.CCRA.L.6—Acquire and use accurately a range of general academic and domain-specific words and phrases sufficient for reading, writing, speaking, and listening at the college and career readiness level; demonstrate independence in gathering vocabulary knowledge when encountering an unknown term important to comprehension or expression.	Vocabulary Sections 1–4; Making Connections Section 2; Culminating Activity

TESOL and WIDA Standards

The lessons in this book promote English language development for English language learners. The following TESOL and WIDA English Language Development Standards are addressed through the activities in this book:

- **Standard 1:** English language learners communicate for social and instructional purposes within the school setting.
- **Standard 2:** English language learners communicate information, ideas and concepts necessary for academic success in the content area of language arts.

Introduction

About the Author—Tedd Arnold

Tedd Arnold was born in Elmira, New York, in 1949. At the age of ten, he moved to Gainesville, Florida, with his family. In Florida he began taking art lessons and eventually went on to graduate from the University of Florida with a degree in fine arts.

Arnold worked for ten years in textbook illustration, graphic design, and advertising. Arnold's wife, Carol, a kindergarten teacher, helped him notice children's books. Arnold was attracted to their colorful pages and the way the pictures and the words went together. Their first son, Walter, inspired his first book, *No Jumping on the Bed!* This book became an International Reading Association–Children's Book Council Children's Choice Book. *No More Water in the Tub!* is a sequel to his first book and was inspired by his second son, William.

Arnold has now published over 60 books as an author and illustrator. His books *Hi! Fly Guy* and *I Spy Fly Guy* have both received the Theodor Seuss Geisel Honor from the American Library Association.

More information about Tedd Arnold and his books can be found at the following website: http://www.teddarnoldbooks.com.

Possible Texts for Text Comparisons

There are 12 other books in this Tedd Arnold series: *Super Fly Guy*; *Shoo, Fly Guy!*; *There Was an Old Lady Who Swallowed Fly Guy*; *Fly High, Fly Guy!*; *Hooray for Fly Guy!*; *I Spy Fly Guy!*; *Fly Guy Meets Fly Girl!*; *Buzz Boy and Fly Guy*; *Fly Guy vs. the Flyswatter!*; *Ride, Fly Guy, Ride!*; *There's a Fly Guy in My Soup*; and *Fly Guy and the Frankenfly*. The series of *Huggly* may also be used for enriching text comparisons by the same author.

Cross-Curricular Connection

This book can be used in a science unit on the study of flies or insects. *Hi! Fly Guy* can also be used in a social studies unit on different kinds of friends.

Introduction

Book Summary of *Hi! Fly Guy*

Hi! Fly Guy is a fun, appealing book that is the first in a series. This book has silly illustrations that draw children in immediately. It all begins when a fly goes looking for something to eat, and a boy is looking for something to catch for the Amazing Pet Show. When the boy catches the fly, he is amazed to find out that the fly calls him by his name—Buzz. Buzz names the fly—Fly Guy. Everyone thinks that flies cannot be pets because they are pests. The judges laugh at Buzz and Fly Guy at the pet show. Fly Guy does some fancy flying and helps prove them all wrong. Fly Guy earns the Smartest Pet ribbon. Buzz learns that Fly Guy is the perfect pet, and a beautiful friendship begins.

Possible Texts for Text Sets

- Bernard, Robin. *Insects.* National Geographic Children's Books, 2001.
- Rabe, Tish. *On Beyond Bugs: All About Insects.* Random House Books for Young Readers, 1999.
- Rockwell, Anne. *Bugs Are Insects.* HarperCollins, 2001.
- Voake, Steve. *Insect Detective.* Candlewick, 2012.

or

- dePaola, Tomie. *Bill and Pete.* Puffin, 1996.
- Hoban, Russell. *A Bargain for Frances.* HarperCollins, 2003.
- Hutchins, Pat. *My Best Friend.* Greenwillow Books, 1993.
- Lobel, Arnold. *Frog and Toad Are Friends.* HarperCollins, 2003.
- Willems, Mo. *There Is a Bird on Your Head!* Disney-Hyperion Books, 2007.

Name _____

Introduction

Pre-Reading Theme Thoughts

Directions: Draw a picture of a happy face or a sad face. Your face should show how you feel about each statement. Then, use words to say what you think about each statement.

Statement	How Do You Feel? 😊 ☹	What Do You Think?
A new pet can make you happy.		
Friends come in all shapes and sizes.		
Flies are pests!		
You should not laugh at others.		

Teacher Plans—Section 1 Chapter 1

Pre-Reading Activities

Pre-Reading Predictions

1. Show students the front and back covers of the book. Read aloud the title. Point out the author. Explain that the author of this book also illustrated the pictures.

2. Explain that good readers make predictions before, during, and after reading. Tell students that a prediction is making a guess about what will happen or what something will be about.

3. Tell students that books are usually literature books or informational texts. Explain that another term for a literature book is fiction and another term for an informational text is nonfiction. Have students share how they can figure out if a book is literature or informational text.

4. Ask students how the fly on the cover looks different from real flies. Ask students if they think this book will be serious or funny.

5. In pairs, have students share their predictions about the book based on the title and the images from the covers.

Pre-Reading Focus—Characters

1. Tell students that there are two characters in this chapter. One is a fly and the other is a boy. Discuss what students already know about flies.

2. Tell students they will need to listen carefully to figure out the boy's name.

3. Have students talk to each other about what they think the fly and the boy are going to do in the story.

Vocabulary Overview

Key words and phrases from this section are provided below with definitions and sentences about how the words are used in the story. Introduce and discuss these important vocabulary words with students. If you think these words or other words in the story warrant more time devoted to them, there are suggestions in the introduction for other vocabulary activities (page 5).

Word	Definition	Sentence about Text
flying (p. 1)	moving through the air with wings	The fly is **flying**.
looking (p. 2)	trying to find something or someone	The fly is **looking** for something to eat.
tasty (p. 2)	having a good flavor; pleasing to taste	The fly wants something **tasty**.
slimy (p. 2)	covered with a thick, slippery liquid	The fly is looking for something **slimy**.
smart (p. 4)	very good at learning or thinking about things	The boy is looking for something **smart**.
met (p. 6)	saw and spoke to someone for the first time	The fly and the boy **met**.
caught (p. 7)	captured and did not allow a person, animal, or fish to escape	The fly is **caught** in a jar.
free (p. 8)	not physically held by something	The fly wants to be **free**.
stomps (p. 8)	to put your foot down forcefully and noisily	The fly **stomps** his foot.
surprised (p. 9)	showed the feeling that people get when something unexpected happens	The boy is **surprised** by the fly.

chapter 1

Name _____

Vocabulary Activity

Directions: Choose at least two words from the story. Draw a picture that shows what these words mean. Label your picture.

Words from the Story

flying	looking	tasty	slimy	smart
met	caught	free	stomps	surprised

Directions: Answer this question.

1. What is the fly **looking** for?

_____

_____

Teacher Plans—Section 1
Chapter 1

Analyzing the Literature

Provided below are discussion questions you can use in small groups, with the whole class, or for written assignments. Each question is written at two levels so you can choose the right question for each group of students. For each question, a few key points are provided for your reference as you discuss the book with students.

Story Element	Level 1	Level 2	Key Discussion Points
Plot	What is the fly looking for?	Describe what the fly is looking for.	The fly is looking for something to eat. He is looking for something tasty and slimy.
Character	Why is the fly mad?	Describe why the fly is mad and how the fly shows he is mad.	The fly is mad because he is in the jar, and he wants to be free. The fly stomps his foot and says, "buzz."
Character	How does the boy feel at the end of the chapter?	What is meaningful about the end of this chapter?	The boy is surprised that the fly knows his name, Buzz. He thinks the fly is the smartest pet in the world.
Setting	What is the setting of this chapter?	Describe the setting of this chapter.	The chapter takes place outside when the boy goes for a walk. Students should use the illustrations to gather information about the setting.

chapter 1

Name _____

Reader Response

Think

In this story, the boy catches the fly in a jar. Think about if you feel it is okay for him to put the fly in a jar.

Opinion Writing Prompt

Write your opinion on whether you think it is a good idea for the boy to put the fly in a jar. Be sure to give reasons for whether it is a good idea or a bad idea.

_____
_____
_____
_____
_____
_____
_____
_____
_____

Name _____

Chapter 1

Guided Close Reading

Carefully reread the last two pages of the chapter (pages 8–9).

Directions: Think about these questions. In the space below, write ideas or draw pictures as you think. Be ready to share your answers.

❶ What text shows how the fly feels?

❷ Look back at the text and describe what the fly does and says.

❸ What word shows how the boy feels at the end of the chapter? Why does he feel this way?

© Shell Education   #40010—Instructional Guide: Hi! Fly Guy   19

chapter 1

Name _____

Making connections—Insects

The fly is an insect. Insects have three body parts. The head is at the top. The thorax is in the middle. The abdomen is behind the thorax.

Directions: Use the words in the Word Box to label the parts of the insect below.

Word Box

abdomen	antennae	eye	head
leg	thorax	wing	

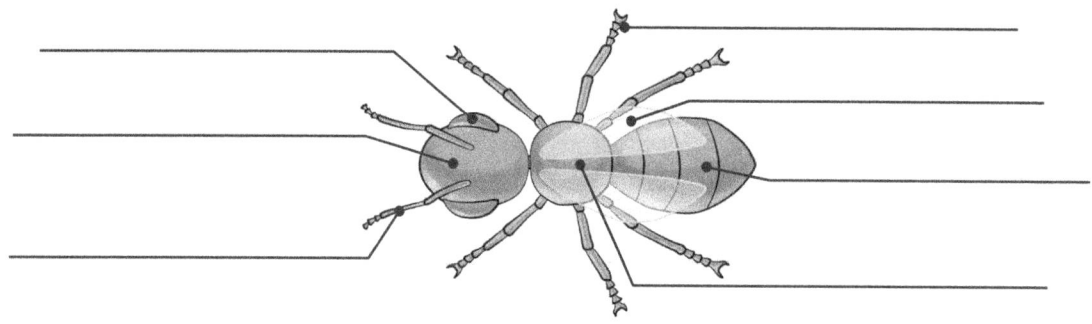

Directions: Use the picture above to fill in the blanks.

1. An insect has _____ antennae.

2. An insect has _____ body parts.

3. An insect has _____ legs.

Name _____

chapter 1

Making Connections—
Fine Arts with Flies

Buzz catches a fly on his walk. You can make your very own pet fly.

Materials
- fly pattern (page 22)
- bubble wrap or wax paper
- glue
- black pipe cleaners cut into 4-inch pieces (8 per student)

Directions: Follow these steps.

1. Color the fly and cut it out.

2. Cut two wings out of bubble wrap or wax paper.

3. Glue the wings on top of the fly.

4. Bend the pipe cleaners into slight "v" shapes.

5. Glue six pipe cleaner legs to the thorax and abdomen of the fly.

6. Glue two pipe-cleaner antennae on the head of the fly.

chapter 1

Making connections— Fine Arts with Flies (cont.)

Name _____

CHAPTER 1

Language Learning— Onomatopoeia Words

Directions: The fly says, "buzz." *Buzz* is an onomatopoeia. This means the word imitates or sounds like a sound. Read the words below and draw a picture of each word in the box.

meow

ding dong

ring

bam

chapter 1

Name _____

Story Elements—Characters

Directions: Think about a pet that you have or would like to have. Write a poem about that pet.

_____

_ _

_____

_ _

_____

_ _

_____

_ _

_____

_ _

_____

_ _

_____

Name _____

chapter 1

Story Elements—Setting

Directions: Draw a picture of the most exciting part of the chapter. In your picture, make sure you show the setting.

chapter 1

Name _____

Story Elements—Plot

Directions: Make a prediction of what will happen next. Write 2–3 sentences describing what you think will happen in the next chapter.

Teacher Plans—Section 2 Chapter 2

Pre-Reading Activities

Pre-Reading Predictions

1. Show students the first two pages of chapter 2.

2. Ask students to make a prediction about the chapter based on the illustrations on the first two pages. Remind them that good readers make predictions before, during, and after reading.

3. Have students share their predictions with partners.

4. Ask students how looking at the illustrations helps them be better readers.

Pre-Reading Focus—Characters

1. Tell students that there are four characters in this chapter. Their names are Buzz, Mom, Dad, and the fly.

2. Have students talk to each other about what they think Buzz, Mom, Dad, and the fly are going to do in the chapter.

3. Tell students they will learn the name of the fly in this chapter.

Teacher Plans—Section 2 Chapter 2

Vocabulary Overview

Key words and phrases from this section are provided below with definitions and sentences about how the words are used in the story. Introduce and discuss these important vocabulary words with students. If you think these words or other words in the story warrant more time devoted to them, there are suggestions in the introduction for other vocabulary activities (page 5).

Word	Definition	Sentence about Text
home (p. 10)	the place such as a house or apartment where a person lives	Buzz takes the fly **home**.
listen (p. 11)	to give attention to a sound	**Listen** as the fly says my name.
opens (p. 11)	to cause something to no longer be covered, sealed, or blocked	Buzz **opens** the jar to let the fly out.
jar (p. 11)	a glass container that has a wide opening and usually a lid	The fly is in the **jar**.
flew out (p. 11)	fled; escaped	The fly **flew out** of the jar.
fly swatter (p. 11)	a device used for killing flies and other insects that has a flat piece of plastic or other material attached to a handle	Dad gets a **fly swatter**.
pests (p. 12)	animals or insects that cause problems for people	Flies are **pests**!
rescue (p. 13)	an act of saving someone or something from danger, harm, or trouble	Buzz comes to the fly's **rescue**.
thought (p. 14)	to use your mind to understand or decide something	Buzz **thought** of a name for the fly.
lunch (p. 15)	a light meal eaten in the middle of the day	Buzz gives Fly Guy some **lunch**.

Name _____

chapter 2

Vocabulary Activity

Directions: Complete each sentence. Use the words listed below.

Words from the Story

home	listen	opens	jar	flew out
pests	fly swatter	rescue	thought	lunch

1. The fly _____ of the _____.

2. The boy comes to _____ the fly.

3. Buzz _____ of a name for the fly.

4. Buzz gives Fly Guy some _____.

Directions: Answer this question.

5. Why does Buzz want Mom and Dad to **listen**?
_____
_____
_____
_____

Teacher Plans—Section 2 chapter 2

Analyzing the Literature

Provided below are discussion questions you can use in small groups, with the whole class, or for written assignments. Each question is written at two levels so you can choose the right question for each group of students. For each question, a few key points are provided for your reference as you discuss the book with students.

Story Element	Level 1	Level 2	Key Discussion Points
Character	Why does Buzz think the fly is smart?	Explain how you know that Buzz thinks the fly is smart.	Buzz thinks the fly is smart because the fly says, "buzz," which is the boy's name.
Plot	Why does Buzz open the jar and let the fly out?	Explain why Buzz opens the jar and lets the fly out. Do you think it was a good idea to let the fly out?	Buzz opens the jar to let the fly out so his mom and dad can hear the fly say his name.
Character	What does Buzz name the fly?	Why does Mom think the fly needs a name?	Mom thinks the fly needs a name because he is a new pet. Buzz names him Fly Guy.
Plot	Why is Fly Guy happy at the end of the chapter?	Describe how Fly Guy feels at the end of the chapter.	Fly Guy is happy because Buzz gives him some lunch. Buzz gives him a hot dog and Fly Guy eats half of it up.

Name _____

Chapter 2

Reader Response

Think

In this story, Fly Guy has a hot dog for lunch. Think about a favorite food you like to eat for lunch.

Narrative Writing Prompt

Write about a food you like eating for lunch. Describe the food and why you enjoy eating it.

_____
_____
_____
_____
_____
_____
_____
_____
_____

chapter 2

Name _____

Guided Close Reading

Closely reread when Dad is chasing Fly Guy (pages 12–13).

Directions: Think about these questions. In the space below, write ideas or draw pictures as you think. Be ready to share your answers.

❶ Use the text to tell what Dad calls flies.

❷ Use the illustrations and the text to describe what Dad uses to chase after the fly.

❸ Find evidence that shows that Dad changes his mind about the fly.

Name _____

Chapter 2

Making connections—Living and Non-Living Things

Directions: Fly Guy is a fly. He is an insect. A fly is a living thing. Buzz is a person, and he is a living thing. The jar is a non-living thing. Draw pictures of living and non-living things in the boxes below. Label your pictures.

Living   **Non-Living**

© Shell Education   #40010—Instructional Guide: Hi! Fly Guy

chapter 2

Name _____

Language Learning— Using Quotation Marks

Directions: Read the sentences below. Use the quotation marks to help you decide what each person is saying. Write what each person is saying in the speech bubbles.

"This is my pet," Buzz said to Mom and Dad. "Flies can't be pets!" said Dad. "They are pests!"

Name _____

chapter 2

Story Elements—Characters

Directions: Reread chapter 2. Look for words or details that give you ideas about the characters. Fill in the chart below.

Character	Character Traits	Details from the Passage
Buzz		
Fly Guy		
Mom		
Dad		

chapter 2

Name _____

Story Elements—Setting

Directions: Draw a picture of the setting with all the characters in this chapter. Label all of the characters.

Teacher Plans—Section 3
Chapter 3

Pre-Reading Activities

Pre-Reading Predictions
1. Show students the first page of chapter 3.
2. Ask students to make predictions based on the illustrations on the first page. Remind them that good readers make predictions before, during, and after reading.
3. Have students share their predictions with partners.

Pre-Reading Focus—Characters
1. Tell students that there are five characters in this chapter—Buzz, Fly Guy, and the three judges.
2. Discuss what *judges* are. Ask students if they have ever been in a contest where there were judges. Have them share any experiences they have had with judges.
3. Have students predict how the judges will act in the story. What will they do and say?

Teacher Plans—Section 3 Chapter 3

Vocabulary Overview

Key words and phrases from this section are provided below with definitions and sentences about how the words are used in the story. Introduce and discuss these important vocabulary words with students. If you think these words or other words in the story warrant more time devoted to them, there are suggestions in the introduction for other vocabulary activities (page 5).

Word	Definition	Sentence about Text
judges (p. 18)	people who decide the winner in a contest or competition	The **judges** laugh at the fly.
sad (p. 20)	not happy; feeling or showing grief or unhappiness	Buzz is **sad** because the judges are laughing.
idea (p. 21)	a thought or plan about what to do	Fly Guy has an **idea** to help Buzz.
fancy (p. 21)	elaborate skill and grace	Fly Guy does some **fancy** tricks.
amazed (p. 22)	feeling or showing great surprise	The judges are **amazed** at the tricks.
tricks (p. 22)	clever and skillful actions performed to entertain or amuse	Fly Guy can do **tricks**.
dived (p. 26)	moved down through the air at a steep angle	Fly Guy **dives** down into the jar.
won (p. 29)	to achieve victory in a fight, contest, game, etc.	Fly Guy **wins** an award.
award (p. 29)	something, such as a prize, that is given for being excellent or for doing something that is admired	Fly Guy wins the **award** for the smartest pet.
beautiful (p. 30)	very good or pleasing; not having bad qualities	Fly Guy and Buzz begin a **beautiful** friendship.

Name _____

chapter 3

Vocabulary Activity

Directions: Practice your vocabulary words and writing skills. Write at least two sentences using words from the story.

Words from the Story

judges	sad	idea	fancy	amazed
tricks	dives	won	award	beautiful

_____

_____

_____

_____

_____

_____

Directions: Answer this question.

1. Why are the **judges amazed**?

_____

_____

_____

Teacher Plans—Section 3 Chapter 3

Analyzing the Literature

Provided below are discussion questions you can use in small groups, with the whole class, or for written assignments. Each question is written at two levels so you can choose the right question for each group of students. For each question, a few key points are provided for your reference as you discuss the book with students.

Story Element	Level 1	Level 2	Key Discussion Points
Character	How do you know that Fly Guy likes Buzz?	Describe the ways that Fly Guy shows Buzz that he likes him.	Fly Guy does some fancy flying for the judges. He also dives down into the jar. Fly Guy does these tricks because he likes Buzz and wants to help him so the judges won't laugh at him.
Plot	What is the problem in this chapter?	Describe the problems in this chapter.	The problem is the judges laugh at Buzz because they believe that flies cannot be pets. Buzz feels sad and lets Fly Guy go.
Setting	What is the setting of this chapter?	The setting of a story is not only what we can see, but also what we can hear. Describe the setting of this chapter.	This story takes place at the Amazing Pet Show. There are many judges and other pets.
Character	What are two words that describe the main character, Buzz?	Describe at least three traits of the main character, Buzz.	Buzz is determined, kind, proud, and even sad at one point in the chapter.

Name _____

Chapter 3

Reader Response

Think

In this story, Buzz and Fly Guy begin a beautiful friendship. Think about a friendship you have with someone.

Narrative Writing Prompt

Write about a friend you have. Give details about what you enjoy doing with your friend and why you like your friend.

chapter 3

Name _____

Guided Close Reading

Closely reread when Fly Guy shows off with fancy flying (pages 20–21).

Directions: Think about these questions. In the space below, write ideas or draw pictures as you think. Be ready to share your answers.

❶ Use the text and illustrations to describe how Buzz is feeling.

❷ Based on the events in the story, why is Buzz feeling this way?

❸ What does Fly Guy do to help Buzz?

Name _____

chapter 3

Making connections—Happy and Sad

Directions: Buzz feels sad when the judges say that flies cannot be pets. Buzz is happy when he wins an award. Draw pictures of how your face looks when you are sad and happy. Write about a time when you have had those feelings.

Feeling Sad	**Feeling Happy**

I feel sad when...
_____

_____

I feel happy when...
_____

_____

chapter 3

Name _____

Making connections—critical Thinking: Pests or Pets?

Directions: Buzz went out looking for a pet. He found a pet that is usually considered a pest. Some animals are pests and some are pets. Some might be both pests and pets. Fill in the Venn diagram below.

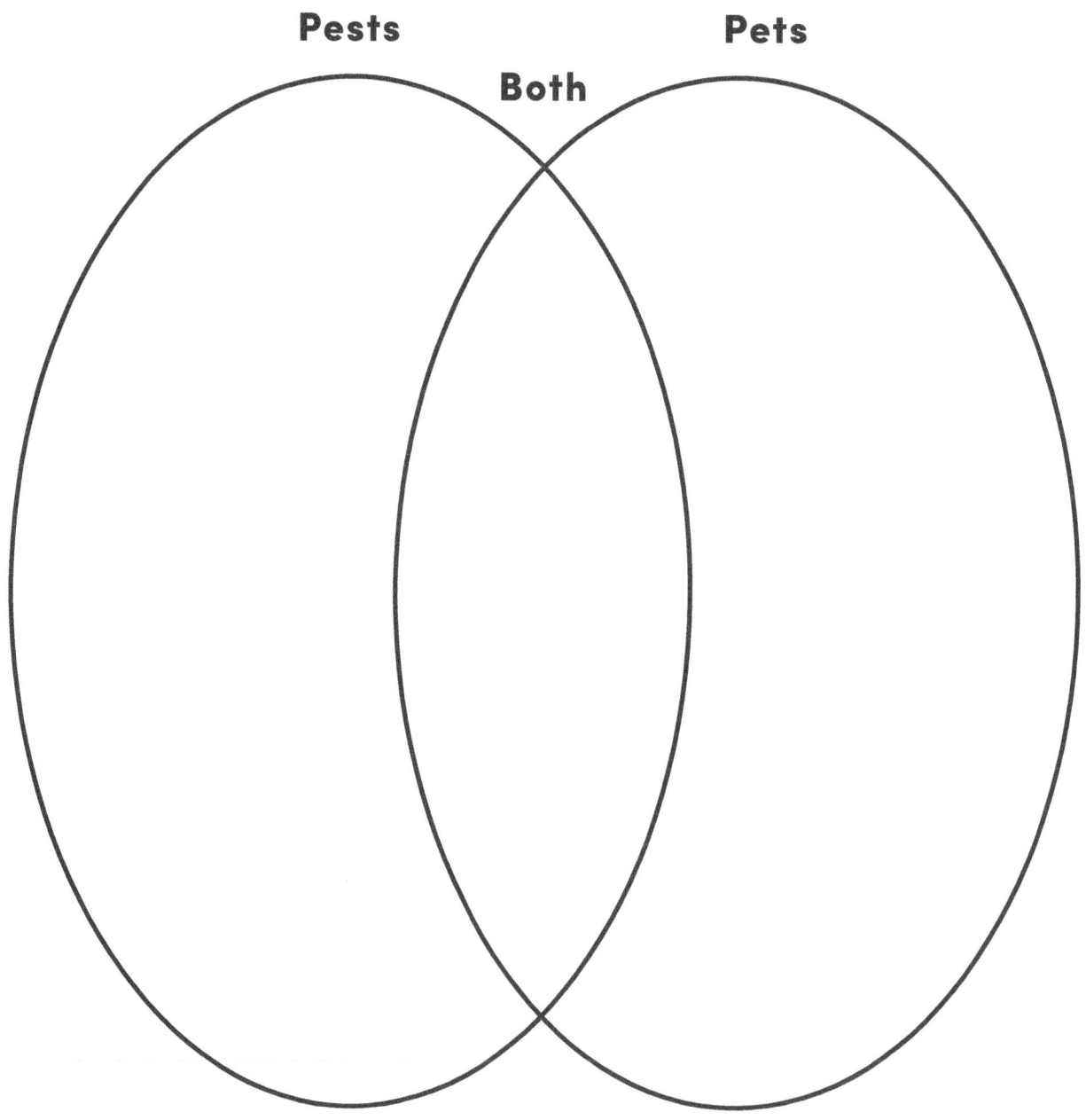

Name _____

Chapter 3

Language Learning—contractions

This chapter uses the contraction **can't**. *Can't* is the shortened form of *cannot*. A contraction is a word that is formed by replacing a missing letter with an apostrophe.

Directions: Color in the shapes below that have contractions in them. Look for a hidden picture!

chapter 3

Name _____

Story Elements–Plot

Directions: Draw three pictures to show the order of events in this chapter. Label each of your pictures.

Name _____

chapter 3

Story Elements—Characters

Directions: Draw a picture of Buzz and Fly Guy having fun together. Write a sentence about your picture.

_____
_____
_____

© Shell Education #40010—Instructional Guide: Hi! Fly Guy

chapter 3

Name _____

Story Elements—Setting

Directions: The setting is where a story takes place. This chapter takes place at a pet show. Draw three things you might see or hear at the pet show. Label each of your pictures.

Teacher Plans—Section 4
Whole Book

Vocabulary Overview

Key words and phrases from the book are provided below with definitions and sentences about how the words are used in the story. This is a good time to discuss the types of words used by the author to make his story come alive. If you think these words or other words in the stories warrant more time devoted to them, there are suggestions in the introduction for other vocabulary activities (page 5).

Word	Definition	Sentence about Text
tasty (p. 2)	having a good flavor; pleasing to taste	The fly wants something **tasty**.
slimy (p. 2)	covered with a thick, slippery liquid	The fly is looking for something **slimy**.
smart (p. 4)	very good at learning or thinking about things	The boy is looking for something **smart**.
jar (p. 11)	a glass container that has a wide opening and usually a lid	The fly is in the **jar**.
pests (p. 12)	animals or insects that cause problems for people	Flies are **pests**!
judges (p. 18)	a person who decides the winner in a contest or competition	The **judges** laugh at the fly.
fancy (p. 21)	elaborate skill and grace	Fly Guy does some **fancy** tricks.
amazed (p. 22)	feeling or showing great surprise	The judges are **amazed** at the tricks.
dived (p. 26)	moved down through the air at a steep angle	Fly Guy **dived** down into the jar.
beautiful (p. 30)	very good or pleasing; not having bad qualities	Fly Guy and Buzz begin a **beautiful** friendship.

Whole Book

Name _____

Vocabulary Activity

Directions: Look back at the whole book, *Hi! Fly Guy*. Choose two words from each chapter that you find interesting or special. Write the words under the boxes below and draw small pictures of those words.

Chapter 1

Chapter 2

Chapter 3

Teacher Plans—Section 4
Whole Book

Analyzing the Literature

Provided below are discussion questions you can use in small groups, with the whole class, or for written assignments. Each question is written at two levels so you can choose the right question for each group of students. For each question, a few key points are provided for your reference as you discuss the book with students.

Story Element	Level 1	Level 2	Key Discussion Points
Character	What do you like best about Buzz?	Describe the best parts of Buzz's character.	Buzz is kind, caring, and clever. He is happy to have a new friend. Buzz is very proud of his accomplishment of winning an award in The Amazing Pet Show.
Plot	What are the problems in this story?	Describe the problems in this story and how they are solved.	There are a few problems in this story. First, the dad says that flies can't be pets and he gets a fly swatter. This problem is solved when the dad thinks the fly is smart because he says, "buzz!" The second problem occurs when the judges laugh and say, "Flies can't be pets." The problem is solved when Fly Guy does some amazing tricks, and he is given the award of Smartest Pet.
Setting	What is your favorite setting in this story?	Describe your favorite setting in this story. Be sure to include everything that you can see, hear, smell, touch, and taste.	Students should share their favorite settings and describe them using their five senses.
Character	What adventures would you like to see Buzz and Fly Guy have?	Tell a story that you think Tedd Arnold should write next about Buzz and Fly Guy.	As long as students have reasons for their responses they are successfully answering the question.

Whole Book

Name _____

Reader Response

Think

In this story, Fly Guy and Buzz win an award at The Amazing Pet Show. Think about how you show good sportsmanship and how to be a good winner or loser.

Informative/ Explanatory Writing Prompt

Write about how to be a good sport when playing a game or when you are in a contest. Give some tips on how to be a good winner or loser.

_____
_____
_____
_____
_____
_____
_____
_____

Name _____

Whole Book

Guided Close Reading

Closely reread when the judges are talking about Fly Guy (pages 22–25).

Directions: Think about these questions. In the space below, write ideas or draw pictures as you think. Be ready to share your answers.

❶ Based on the events in the story, why are the judges amazed?

❷ Use the book to tell what they say flies can't be.

❸ Looking back at the text, how did Fly Guy fly into the sky?

Whole Book

Name _____

Making Connections— Friendships Are Fun!

Directions: Buzz and Fly Guy begin a beautiful friendship in this book. Draw a picture of you doing something fun with a friend. Write a sentence about your picture.

Name _____

Whole Book

Language Learning—Adjectives

This story uses many adjectives. Adjectives are words that describe things.

Directions: Read the adjectives from the story in the Word Box. Write your own sentences using at least three of these adjectives.

Word Box

tasty	slimy	smart	mad
happy	sad	beautiful	fancy

1. _____

2. _____

3. _____

Whole Book

Name _____

Story Elements—Characters

Directions: Write two alliterative sentences that describe Buzz in this story. An alliterative sentence has most words that start with the same letter. That means that most of the words in your sentences need to begin with the letter **b**.

Name _____

Whole Book

Story Elements—Plot

Directions: Write a new chapter for this book. Buzz and Fly Guy are now friends. What adventure might they have next?

Post-Reading Activities

Post-Reading Theme Thoughts

Directions: Choose a main character from *Hi! Fly Guy*. Pretend you are that character. Draw a picture of a happy face or a sad face to show how the character would feel about each statement. Then, use words to explain your picture.

Character I Chose _____

Statement	How Does the Character Feel? 😊 ☹	Explain How the Character Feels
A new pet can make you happy.		
Friends come in all shapes and sizes.		
Flies are pests!		
You should not laugh at others.		

Post-Reading Activities

Culminating Activity: The Adventures of Fly Guy and Buzz

Directions: Work with students to help them choose one of the following activities. Most likely, these activities will require adult assistance to complete. The stick puppets on pages 59–61 may be fun for students to use as they perform these different activities.

- Have students write and illustrate their own Buzz and Fly Guy adventures. They should base the stories on their own experiences with friends. For example, they could write *Buzz and Fly Guy Go to the Park* or *Buzz and Fly Guy Meet a New Friend*. They can use the stick puppets on pages 59–61 to perform their scripts. If other characters are needed, students can make new stick puppets.

- Have students prepare the stick puppets to use with the reader's theater script on pages 62–64. Let small groups of students take turns reading the parts and using the stick puppets.

- As a class or in small groups, recreate the winners of The Amazing Pet Show. Explain that the words *tallest*, *heaviest*, *smartest*, and *cutest* are used when three or more things are compared. Also the word *most* is used to describe these comparisons. Have students draw the animals on pages 28–29 of *Hi! Fly Guy* on pieces of construction paper. Encourage students to also draw different pets that might win awards at the show. Have students create a pet parade around the classroom. You may wish to hang the pets in the classroom as a bulletin board display.

Fly Guy

Post-Reading Activities

Culminating Activity: The Adventures of Fly Guy and Buzz *(cont.)*

Directions: Reproduce the stick puppet patterns on tagboard or construction paper. Have students cut them along the dashed lines. To complete the stick puppets, glue each pattern to a tongue depressor or craft stick.

Mom   **Buzz**

Culminating Activity: The Adventures of Fly Guy and Buzz (cont.)

Post-Reading Activities

Narrator

Dad

Post-Reading Activities

Culminating Activity: Reader's Theater—Fly Guy Goes to the Fair (cont.)

Characters
- Narrator
- Buzz
- Fly Guy
- Dad
- Mom

Narrator: A boy has a pet fly named Fly Guy. Fly Guy can say the boy's name.

Fly Guy: Buzz!

Narrator: One day, Mom and Dad tell Buzz they are going to the fair.

Buzz: Hooray! We're going to the fair!

Fly Guy: Fairz!

Dad: Let's get in the car.

Buzz: Fly Guy wants to go, too.

Mom: He's too little. He might get lost.

Buzz: Please!

Fly Guy: Pleaze!

Culminating Activity: Reader's Theater—Fly Guy Goes to the Fair (cont.)

Dad: Okay.

Narrator: The family drives to the fair.

Mom: We're here!

Buzz: Hooray! Let's go, Fly Guy!

Fly Guy: Okayz!

Mom: First, we'll have lunch.

Dad: Let's get a hot dog.

Buzz: Fly Guy wants to go eat out of the trash.

Narrator: Fly Guy flies to the trash can, but something else catches his eye. It is cotton candy.

Fly Guy: Yummz!

Narrator: Fly Guy flies straight into a little boy's cotton candy. Fly Guy is caught in the cotton candy.

Fly Guy: Oopz! Ztickeez! Ztickeez!

Post-Reading Activities

Culminating Activity: Reader's Theater—Fly Guy Goes to the Fair (cont.)

Narrator: The little boy throws his cotton candy away.

Buzz: Where's Fly Guy?

Dad: Mom said he might get lost.

Narrator: Buzz hears a noise coming from the trash can.

Fly Guy: Buzz! Buzz!

Mom: I think he's in the trash can.

Narrator: Buzz looks into the trash can. Fly Guy is stuck in the cotton candy.

Fly Guy: Buzz! Buzz!

Buzz: Fly Guy!

Narrator: Buzz pulls Fly Guy off the cotton candy.

Buzz: I am so glad I found you!

Dad: Now, let's go have some more fun!

Fly Guy: Fairz!

Name _____

Post-Reading Activities

Comprehension Assessment

Directions: Fill in the bubble for the best response to each question.

Chapter 1

1. Why does the boy go for a walk?

    - Ⓐ The boy is surprised.
    - Ⓑ He wants to be free.
    - Ⓒ He is looking for something to catch.
    - Ⓓ He is looking for something to eat.

2. Describe why the boy is surprised at the end of the chapter.

    _____
    _____
    _____
    _____

Chapter 2

3. How does the author show that Dad changes his mind about the fly?

    - Ⓐ "Flies can't be pets!"
    - Ⓑ "This fly is smart!"
    - Ⓒ "They are pests!"
    - Ⓓ "Buzz!"

Post-Reading Activities

Comprehension Assessment (cont.)

Chapter 3

4. What shows why Buzz is sad?

   - Ⓐ Fly Guy does some fancy flying.
   - Ⓑ Fly Guy flies high, high, high into the sky.
   - Ⓒ The judges let Fly Guy in the show.
   - Ⓓ The judges laugh.

Whole Book

5. Explain why the judges are amazed by Fly Guy.

_____

_____

_____

_____

_____

_____

Name _____

Post-Reading Activities

Response to Literature: Fly Guy and Buzz Meet

Directions: Choose one scene from any of the *Hi! Fly Guy* chapters you've read. Think about which scene is your favorite. Draw a picture of that scene. Then, answer the questions on the next page. Make sure your picture is neat and is in color.

Post-Reading Activities

Name _____

Response to Literature: Fly Guy and Buzz Meet (cont.)

1. What is happening in the scene?

   _____
   _____
   _____
   _____
   _____

2. Why did you choose this scene?

   _____
   _____
   _____
   _____
   _____

3. What happens next in the story?

   _____
   _____
   _____
   _____

Name _____

Post-Reading Activities

Response to Literature Rubric

Directions: Use this rubric to evaluate student responses.

Great Job	Good Work	Keep Trying
☐ You answered all three questions completely. You included many details.	☐ You answered all three questions.	☐ You did not answer all three questions.
☐ Your handwriting is very neat. There are no spelling errors.	☐ Your handwriting can be neater. There are some spelling errors.	☐ Your handwriting is not very neat. There are many spelling errors.
☐ Your picture is neat and fully colored.	☐ Your picture is neat and some of it is colored.	☐ Your picture is not very neat and/or fully colored.
☐ Creativity is clear in both the picture and the writing.	☐ Creativity is clear in either the picture or the writing.	☐ There is not much creativity in either the picture or the writing.

Teacher Comments: _____

_____

_____

_____

Writing Paper

Name _____

Answer Key

The responses provided here are just examples of what students may answer. Many accurate responses are possible for the questions throughout this unit.

Vocabulary Activity—Section 1: Chapter 1 (page 16)

1. The fly is **looking** for something **tasty** and **slimy**.

Guided Close Reading—Section 1: Chapter 1 (page 19)

1. The words "mad" and "wanted to be free" are used.
2. The fly stomps his feet and says, "buzz."
3. The boy is surprised because the fly says, "buzz," and he thinks the fly knows his name.

Making Connections—Section 1: Chapter 1 (page 20)

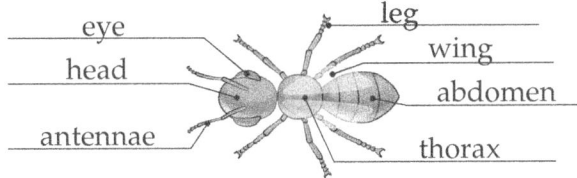

1. 2
2. 3
3. 6

Story Elements—Plot—Section 1: Chapter 1 (page 26)

- Students' responses will vary, but should be a written prediction of what they think will happen in the next chapter. Look for predictions based on what has happened so far in the story rather than wild guesses.

Vocabulary Activity—Section 2: Chapter 2 (page 29)

1. The fly **flew out** of the **jar**.
2. The boy comes to **rescue** the fly.
3. Buzz **thought** of a name for the fly.
4. Buzz gives Fly Guy some **lunch**.
5. Buzz wants Mom and Dad to **listen** to the fly say Buzz's name.

Guided Close Reading—Section 2: Chapter 2 (page 32)

1. Dad calls the flies "pests."
2. Dad uses the fly swatter.
3. Dad says the fly is smart.

Making Connections—Section 2: Chapter 2 (page 33)

- Drawings will vary, but should include correctly labeled living things and non-living things in the two columns.

Language Learning—Section 2: Chapter 2 (page 34)

- The following sentence should be in the speech bubble above Buzz: **This is my pet.**
- The following sentences should be in the speech bubble above Dad: **Flies can't be pets! They are pests!**

Story Elements—Section 2: Chapter 2 (page 35)

- Character traits and supporting details will vary, but might include:

Character	Character Traits	Details from the Passage
Buzz	giving	"Buzz gave Fly Guy something to eat."
Fly Guy	smart	"He can say my name."
Mom	nice	"He needs a name."
Dad	angry	"They are pests!"

Vocabulary Activity—Section 3: Chapter 3 (page 39)

1. The **judges** are **amazed** because the fly can do tricks, knows the boy's name, and knows his jar.

Guided Close Reading—Section 3: Chapter 3 (page 42)

1. Buzz is feeling "sad."
2. Buzz is feeling sad because the judges are laughing at him.
3. Fly Guy has an idea to do some fancy flying tricks.

Answer Key

Making Connections—Section 3: Chapter 3 (page 43)
- Drawings will vary, but should show something happy and sad. The sentences should be completed.

Making Connections—Section 3: Chapter 3 (page 44)
- Venn diagram should be filled with animals that are pests, pets, and some that are considered both.

Language Learning—Section 3: Chapter 3 (page 45)

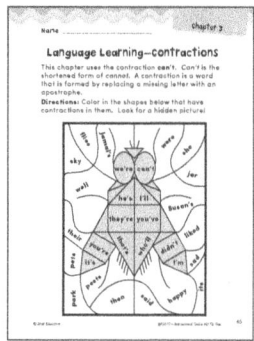

Story Elements—Section 3: Chapter 3 (page 46)
- Drawings will vary, but should show three events in the correct order and be correctly labeled.

Vocabulary Activity—Section 4: Whole Book (page 50)
- Words and pictures will vary, but should show their understanding of the words they choose.

Guided Close Reading—Section 4: Whole Book (page 53)
1. The judges are amazed the fly can do tricks and knows the boy's name.
2. Flies can't be pets.
3. "Fly Guy flew high, high, high into the sky."

Making Connections—Section 4: Whole Book (page 54)
- Drawings will vary, but should show friends doing something fun and a sentence to describe the picture.

Language Learning—Section 4: Whole Book (page 55)
- Sentences will vary, but should include three adjectives used correctly.

Story Elements—Section 4: Whole Book (page 56)
- Sentences will vary, but should have sentences about Buzz where most of the words begin with the letter *b*.

Story Elements—Section 4: Whole Book (page 57)
- Students' writings will vary, but should include a description of a new chapter of the book.

Comprehension Assessment (pages 65–66)
1. C. He is looking for something to catch.
2. The boy is surprised because the fly says, "buzz!" The boy thinks the fly knows his name, Buzz.
3. B. "This fly is smart."
4. D. The judges laugh.
5. The judges are amazed because the fly can do tricks, knows the boy's name, and knows his jar.

www.ingramcontent.com/pod-product-compliance
Lightning Source LLC
Chambersburg PA
CBHW081402290426
44110CB00018B/2456